CHRISTMAS JOKES

SANDY RANSFORD has been hooked on humour ever since her first job in publishing – editing the jokes for a well-known magazine – and she has now written more joke books than she can count. Born in South Yorkshire (which may account for it), she now lives in rural mid-Wales surrounded by sheep, with her husband, a horse, a cat, two pygmy goats and two miniature ponies – all of which keep her laughing.

JANE ECCLES is a prolific and talented illustrator. She lives in London with her husband, her son Theo and a great many plants. She is also hoping to adopt a rescue cat.

Also published by Macmillan

Pony Puzzles
Diana Kimpton

Pony Crosswords
Roy and Sue Preston

He Shoots, He Scores
30 Football Crosswords
Roy and Sue Preston

Football Jokes
Sandy Ransford

Football Puzzles
Sandy Ransford

The Knock Knock Joke Book
Sandy Ransford

2001: A Joke Odyssey
The Millennium Joke Book
Sandy Ransford

Spooky Jokes
Sandy Ransford

CHRISTMAS JOKES

Sandy Ransford

ILLUSTRATED BY
Jane Eccles

MACMILLAN CHILDREN'S BOOKS

First published 1999 by Macmillan Children's Books

This edition produced 2001 for
The Book People Ltd, Hall Wood Avenue,
Haydock, St Helens WA11 9UL

ISBN 0 330 37522 9

3 5 7 9 8 6 4

A CIP catalogue record for this book is available from the British Library.

Printed by Mackays of Chatham plc, Chatham, Kent.

CONTENTS

HANG UP YOUR STOCKING

What's the best present for someone who likes to play it cool?
A combined fridge and CD player.

ANNIE: Why do you want a compass for Christmas?
DANNY: So I know whether I'm coming or going.

GEMMA: First the good news – Mum gave me a goldfish for Christmas.
EMMA: What's the bad news?
GEMMA: I get the bowl next Christmas.

LIZZIE: Mum, do you remember that plate Granny gave you last Christmas and that you were so worried we might break?
MOTHER: Yes.
LIZZIE: Well, your worries are over.

SHANE: How are you getting on with the guitar your dad gave you for Christmas?
WAYNE: Oh, I threw it away.
SHANE: Why did you do that?
WAYNE: It had a hole in the middle.

Little Belinda was given a bottle of perfume and a recorder for Christmas. Her parents' rather pompous friends arrived for lunch on Boxing Day, and as the family sat down at the table, Belinda confided to them, 'If you smell a little smell, and hear a little noise, it's me.'

What's the best Christmas present?
Difficult to say, but a drum takes a lot of beating.

BABY SKUNK: Can I have a chemistry set for Christmas?
MOTHER SKUNK: What, and stink the house out?

FIRST SPIDER: What shall I buy my husband for Christmas?
SECOND SPIDER: Buy him what I bought mine – four pairs of socks.

What did the Christmas stocking say when it had a hole in it?
'Well, I'll be darned!'

FLOYD: I forgot to send Uncle Fred a Christmas card.
LLOYD: What did he say?
FLOYD: Nothing yet.

ERIC: I was going to buy you some hankies for Christmas.
UNCLE DEREK: Why didn't you?
ERIC: I couldn't find any big enough for your nose.

BARRY: I like your new Christmas bike but why are its tyres flat?
LARRY: So my feet can reach the pedals.

RYAN: We were given a cat for Christmas and told it would purr more than any other cat.
BRYAN: Why was that?
RYAN: It was a Purrsian cat.

DAD: Would you like a pocket calculator for Christmas?
DENNIS: No, thanks, I already know how many pockets I've got.

MRS LARGE: If I were you I'd ask for an automatic dishwasher for Christmas.
MRS WIDE: But we don't have automatic dishes.

What can you give a deaf fisherman for Christmas?
A herring aid.

LITTLE LENNY: I want a choo-choo for Christmas, a choo-choo, a choo-choo.
MOTHER: Are you catching a cold, dear?

MR PEEDY: Has that book on body-building you were given last Christmas had any effect yet?
MR WEEDY: Yes, now I can lift the book above my head.

MRS WADDLE: Your husband seems to be a man of rare gifts.
MRS TWADDLE: Yes, it's years since I had a Christmas present.

MOTHER: Why are you crying?
ARABELLA: Jennifer broke my doll.
MOTHER: How did she do that?
ARABELLA: I hit her over the head with it.

A lady walking down the street found a little boy crying. 'What's the matter?' she asked.

'I was given a puppy for Christmas and I swapped him with my friend for a cake his granny had made,' answered the boy.

'And now you wish you hadn't?' asked the lady.

'Yes,' sobbed the lad.

'Because you loved your puppy and realize how much you miss him?' asked the lady.

'No,' said the boy. 'Because I've finished the cake and now I'm hungry again.'

TILLY: Why do you call your puppy Camera?
MILLY: Because he snaps a lot.

GILLY: I was given a pony for Christmas. Would you like to come and see her?
BILLY: Does she bite?
GILLY: That's what I want you to help me find out.

BEN: Did you like the dictionary I gave you for Christmas?
LEN: Yes, I've been trying to find the words to thank you.

CHERYL: What's your new perfume called?
BERYL: High Heaven.
CHERYL: It certainly smells to it!

HARRY (HANDING OVER A BOX OF CHOCOLATES): Here's your Christmas present. Sweets to the sweet.
HETTIE: Thanks. Have a nut.

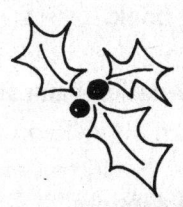

What do you call a little lobster who won't share his toys?
Shellfish.

Knock, knock.
Who's there?
Harvey.
Harvey who?
Harvey going to open our presents yet?

FREDDIE: You gave me this car for Christmas and it won't go up hills.
UNCLE BERT: On the level, it's a good car.

MARTIN: Why did your dad get splinters from the book you gave him for Christmas?
MERVYN: It was a log book.

MARY: I'm giving my dad banana skins for Christmas.
CARY: Banana skins?
MARY: Yes, a pair of slippers.

What's harder than a diamond for Christmas?
Paying for it!

A lady went into a pet shop to buy a bird for her husband's Christmas present.

She pointed to one brightly-coloured creature. 'That's a nice-looking bird,' she said. 'What is it?'

'That, madam, is a gobble bird,' replied the shop assistant. 'Look, I'll show you what it does.' And he waved a pen at the gobble bird and said, 'Gobble bird, my pen', and the bird flew down, picked up the pen, and ate it. Then he said, 'Gobble bird, my hanky', and the gobble bird grabbed his hanky from his pocket and ate that, too.

'How amazing,' said the customer. And she bought the gobble bird, took it home, and gave it to her husband on Christmas Day. He had never seen a gobble bird before, so his wife explained what it did.

'I don't believe a word of it,' snorted her husband. 'Gobble bird, my foot . . .'

SAMANTHA: You've written a cheque for £100.
SELINA: It's a Christmas present for my brother.
SAMANTHA: But you haven't signed it.
SELINA: No, I'm sending it anonymously.

DAD: What have you got your eye on for Christmas?
DENNIS: I've got my eye on that shiny red bike in the shop in the high street.
DAD: Well, you'd better keep your eye on it, because you'll never get your bottom on it.

SHOPPING SPREE

JIMMY: Did you really manage to buy your girlfriend a diamond ring for £2.50?
TIMMY: Yes. It didn't have a stone in it, though.

MAN IN SHOP: I'm trying to buy a present for my wife. Can you help me out?
SHOP ASSISTANT: Certainly, sir. Which way did you come in?

MR CRISP: I bought my wife a bottle of toilet water for Christmas. It cost me £25.
MR NUT: You should have come round to our house. You could have had water out of our toilet for nothing.

MRS FEATHER: How much are those teddy bears?
SHOP ASSISTANT: £9 the pair or £5 for one.
MRS FEATHER: Here's £4 – I'll have the other one.

Which bear got off the train at the wrong London station and never became famous?
Euston Bear.

MRS FLIVVER: Have you any crocodile shoes?
SHOP ASSISTANT: Certainly, madam. What size feet does your crocodile have?

A lady went into a knitting-wool shop and said to the assistant, 'I'm going to knit my little dog a coat for Christmas but I'm not sure how much wool I'll need.'

'Why don't you bring him in and we'll measure him and work it out,' suggested the assistant.

'Oh, I couldn't do that!' exclaimed the shopper. 'You see, I want it to be a surprise.'

Silly Billy was spending his Christmas gift voucher at a clothing shop. After spending some time looking around, he said, 'I'd like a blue shirt to match my eyes.'

'I'm afraid we don't have any blue shirts,' replied the assistant. 'But we do have some soft hats that would match your head.'

Mrs Grey asked Mrs White if she'd see how much suitcases were when she went shopping. Mrs White wasn't sure quite what Mrs Grey wanted, so she looked at each suitcase the shop had in turn, opening it and looking inside before going on to the next one. When she had looked at every suitcase except one, she realized the shop assistant's eyes were on her. 'Oh,' she explained, 'I'm not buying anything just now, I'm looking for a friend.'

'Go ahead and look in that one too if you think she'll be in there,' drawled the assistant.

WOMAN SHOPPER: I'd like to buy my husband a shirt for Christmas.
SHOP ASSISTANT: Certainly, madam. What collar size?
WOMAN SHOPPER: I'm not sure, but I can just get both my hands round his neck.

JANE: I wish I could afford to buy a pedigree puppy for Christmas.
WAYNE: Why do you want a pedigree puppy?
JANE: Oh I don't want one, I just wish I had enough money to buy one.

A woman went into a pet shop to buy her husband a present and chose a parrot. 'That's a very special parrot,' said the shop assistant. 'If you pull the ribbon round its right foot it sings "Jingle Bells", if you pull the ribbon round its left foot it sings "Silent Night".'

'Gosh,' said the woman. 'What happens if I pull both ribbons at the same time?'

'I fall off the perch, stupid,' snarled the parrot.

A man went into a very expensive fruit and vegetable shop and asked for a pound of apples. 'That'll be £2.50,' said the shop assistant.

'£2.50!' exclaimed the man. 'It's daylight robbery!' Nevertheless he handed the assistant £3 and began to walk out of the shop.

'Hang on,' called out the assistant, 'you've forgotten your change.'

'You'd better keep it,' said the man. 'I trod on a grape on the way in.'

The department head in a store found one of his saleswomen arguing with a customer, so he took her on one side and told her she must never argue – the customer was always right. 'Yes,' agreed the saleswoman.

'Well, what were you arguing about?' asked the department manager.

'Actually, it was about you,' she replied. 'The customer said you were a fool, and I said you weren't.'

DUMB DONALD: I'd like to buy a puppy for my brother. How much are they?
PET SHOP OWNER: £25 apiece.
DUMB DONALD: How much is a whole one?

SILLY BILLY: How much are your £10 shoes?
SMART SALESMAN: £5 a foot.

Did you hear about the tragedy at the supermarket? A customer was leaning over the frozen foods counter to reach the Christmas turkeys when five fish fingers reached up and strangled him.

What did Mr Tightfist buy Mrs Tightfist for Christmas when she said she wanted a trip round the world?
A globe.

Neddie kept asking for a video for Christmas but his parents said they couldn't afford one. But on Christmas Eve he came staggering home with a large parcel, and when he unpacked it his parents saw it was a video. 'But where did you get the money from to buy it?' asked his mum.

'No problem about that,' replied Neddie. 'I sold the television.'

Carol was looking for a Christmas card for her boyfriend. She couldn't find quite the right thing, until the saleswoman showed her one that read, 'To the only boy I've ever loved.'

'That's just right,' said Carol. 'I'll take half a dozen, please.'

MAUREEN: My dad spent Christmas in jail — they caught him doing his Christmas shopping early.
DOREEN: But why does doing your shopping early get you arrested?
MAUREEN: He was caught in the jeweller's at two in the morning.

SANTA BANTER

How does Santa dress in the middle of winter?
Quickly!

How many chimneys does Santa have to climb down?
Stacks.

Why *does* Santa climb down chimneys?
Because it soots him.

What exams did Santa pass when he was at school?
Ho, ho, ho levels.

How many presents can Santa fit into an empty sack measuring two metres by one metre?
Only one – after that it isn't empty any more.

On which side of Santa's face is his beard?
The outside.

The father of one of Santa's elves was worried because his son spent a lot of money gambling. He asked Santa to help him solve his son's problem, and one day Santa came to the father elf and told him he thought he'd cured his son. 'Really?' said the father. 'What did you do?'

'I caught him staring at my beard,' replied Santa. 'He said, "Is your beard real or false? I bet you £5 it's false." So I let him pull it to show it was real, and took the £5 off him.'

'Oh dear,' said the elf's father. 'He bet me £10 he'd pull your beard.'

What do Santa's elves say when they get back to Lapland after delivering the presents on Christmas Eve?
'Gnome, sweet gnome.'

Who takes presents to pussy cats?
Santa Claws.

Who takes presents to man-eating tigers?
Santa Jaws.

ANNIE: What does Santa do in the summer?
DANNY: He's a gardener.
ANNIE: How do you know that?
DANNY: Because he's always saying, 'Hoe, hoe, hoe.'

TERRY: The Santa at the store had a really bushy beard.
KERRY: Naval?
TERRY: No, it was on his chin.

What's Santa's wife called?
Mary Christmas.

What do you call a letter Santa has dropped down the chimney?
Blackmail.

What's red and white, bounces and goes 'ho, ho, ho'?
Santa on a pogo stick.

TILLY: One year Santa wasn't feeling well.
MILLY: Why was that?
TILLY: He was wearing gloves.

Why did Santa spring back
up the chimney?
To try out his new jump suit.

Santa and his elves were up on a roof one
Christmas Eve when a young elf insisted on
walking along the ridge tiles. 'You'll fall and hurt
yourself,' said Santa. 'Come down.'

'No,' replied the elf. 'It's fun up here.'

'Very well,' said Santa. 'But if you fall and
break your legs don't come running to me.'

Santa's elves were remembering one very cold Christmas. 'I couldn't feel my fingers or toes for a week,' said one.

'Nor could I,' agreed another. 'It was so cold Santa's teeth were chattering when they weren't even in his mouth.'

What do Santa's elves have for tea?
Fairy cakes.

JIMMY: Did you hear what happened when Santa advertised for a wife?
TIMMY: No, what?
JIMMY: He had 20 replies.
TIMMY: Were they any good?
JIMMY: Well, they all said you can have mine.

Did you hear about the idiot who asked Santa for a packet of birdseed? 'What kind of birds have you got?' he replied. 'None,' responded the idiot, 'but I'd like to grow some.'

Is Santa fat?
Fat? He had mumps for a fortnight before anyone realized!

What's red and white, goes 'ho, ho, ho' and spins round and round?
Santa in a washing machine.

MIKE: When I was young
we lived in a really tough
neighbourhood.
SPIKE: Really?
MIKE: Yes. One year I
hung up my Christmas
stocking and Santa stole it.

Knock, knock.
Who's there?
Felix.
Felix who?
Felix cited about Santa
coming on Christmas Eve.

Why is Santa's nose in the middle of his face?
Because it's the scenter.

Where was Santa when the lights went out?
In the dark.

What nationality is Santa?
North Polish.

What's the last thing Santa takes off before he
goes to bed on Christmas Eve?
His feet off the floor.

How can you thank Santa for bringing your presents?
With a round of Sant-applause.

Why does Mrs Santa wear rollers in her hair in bed on Christmas Eve?
So she'll wake up curly in the morning.

What happened when Santa's dog ate garlic?
His bark was worse than his bite.

What happened when Mrs Santa served soapflakes instead of cornflakes for breakfast?
Santa was so angry he foamed at the mouth.

What kind of coat does Santa wear when it's raining on Christmas Eve?
A wet one.

MERRY CHRISTMAS, DEER

What's the wettest animal in the world?
A reindeer.

How do you make a slow reindeer fast?
Don't feed him.

Why are reindeer such bad dancers?
They have two left feet.

What do you call a reindeer with a number plate on its rump?
Reg.

What does a reindeer say before telling you a joke?
'This one'll sleigh you.'

What game do four reindeer play in the back of a Mini?
Squash.

Dancer the reindeer was always asking questions and Santa got a bit fed up with him. 'Remember,' said Santa, 'curiosity killed the cat.'

'Really?' said Dancer. 'What was it trying to find out?'

What do you get if you cross a reindeer with a plank of wood?
A hat rack.

BRYN: Did you hear the story of the three reindeer?
GWYN: No.
BRYN: Oh dear, dear, dear.

Mr and Mrs Crabby were on holiday in Russia, with a guide called Rudolph showing them all the sights. Mr Crabby was always arguing with him. When they arrived in front of the Kremlin Mr Crabby said, 'Look, it's snowing.'

Rudolph disagreed. 'No, it's raining.'

'Rubbish,' said Mr Crabby. 'That's not rain, it's snow.'

'I'm afraid you're wrong,' persisted Rudolph. 'It's rain.'

Mr Crabby was about to argue again when Mrs Crabby, who was getting fed up with it all, butted in. 'I think you'll find,' she said, 'that Rudolph the Red knows rain, dear.'

JENNY: Are you having Rudolph for Christmas dinner?
BENNY: No, a turkey as usual.

What do you call a reindeer with one eye?
No idea (No-eye deer).

TOMMY: How many legs does Rudolph have?
TAMMY: Four.
TOMMY: No, six.
TAMMY: How come?
TOMMY: He has forelegs in front and two behind.

Overheard one Christmas Eve: 'I don't care who you are, fat man – just get those reindeer off my roof!'

What runs round Santa's reindeer paddock without moving?
The fence.

What music could the reindeer hear in their field?
Pop corn.

What do polar bears eat for lunch?
Ice-burgers.

What's the cheapest pet to feed?
A polar bear – it lives on ice.

Why do polar bears wear white fur coats?
They'd look silly in plastic macs.

Where does a ten-foot high polar bear sleep?
Anywhere it wants to.

A polar bear cub was talking to its mother at the North Pole. 'Mum,' he asked, 'am I a real polar bear?'

'Yes, of course you are,' she replied. 'Why do you ask?'

'Because I'm absolutely freezing!'

GAME WARDEN: What are you doing with that gun?
TOURIST: Hunting polar bears.
GAME WARDEN: But there aren't any polar bears round here.
TOURIST: No, that's why I'm hunting for them.

FREEZE
A JOLLY GOOD
FELLOW

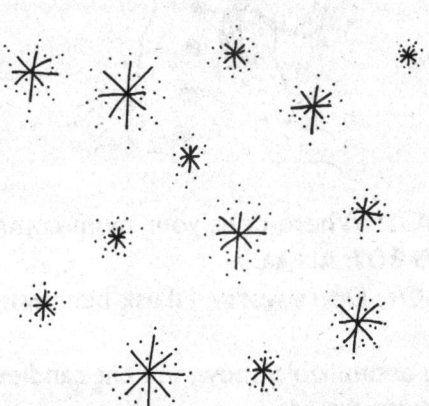

What do people sing at an abominable
snowman's birthday party?
'Freeze a jolly good fellow.'

Why is it hard to keep a secret at the North
Pole?
Because your teeth chatter.

What do snowmen call their money?
Iced lolly.

FIRST BOY: Where does your mum come from?
SECOND BOY: Alaska.
FIRST BOY: Don't worry, I'll ask her myself.

Why do abominable snowmen eat candles?
For light refreshment.

How did the abominable snowman know his
engagement was off?
His girlfriend gave him the cold shoulder.

An Eskimo mother was reading her little boy a bedtime story. 'Little Jack Horner sat in the corner . . .'

'Mum,' interrupted her son, 'what's a corner?'

What's an ig?
An Eskimo house without a loo.

What did the boy say to the girl when they met at the North Pole?
'What's an ice girl like you doing in a place like this?'

What did the north wind say to the east wind?
'Let's play draughts.'

What's a mushroom?
A place where Eskimos keep their huskies.

Knock, knock.
Who's there?
Victor.
Victor who?
Victor his trousers on the ice.

HARRY: I'm so unlucky my plastic flowers wilted.
LARRY: I'm so unlucky my stuffed bird migrated.
BARRY: That's nothing. I went skating and the ice rink caught fire.

MOTHER: Scrape that mud and slush off your shoes before you come into the kitchen.
LIONEL: But, Mother, I'm not wearing any shoes.

MOTHER: Harold! Have you put your boots on yet?
HAROLD: Yes, Mum – all except one.

BRENDA: During the long, dark nights last winter I dressed all in white so the traffic could see me when I walked down the road.
GLENDA: Did it work?
BRENDA: No, I was knocked down by a snowplough.

FARMER GILES: I think it's going to snow.
FARMER MILES: How do you know?
FARMER GILES: When I milked the cows I got ice cream.

What's white and flies upwards?
A silly snowflake.

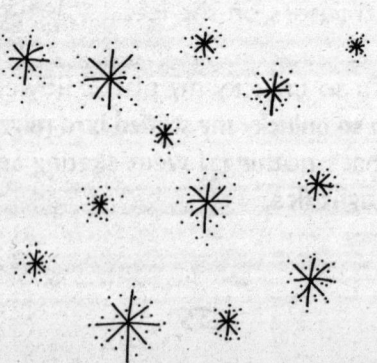

How do sheep keep warm at the North Pole?
Central bleating.

What sort of sheet can't be folded?
A sheet of ice.

What happens when you slip on ice?
Your bottom gets thaw.

PATTY: It's raining cats and dogs.
MATTIE: I know, I just stepped in a poodle.

What's worse than raining cats and dogs?
Hailing taxis.

Why did the snow drop?
Because it heard the crow cuss.

What often falls at the North Pole but never
gets hurt?
Snow.

What has a trunk and is found at the North
Pole?
A lost elephant.

What's the cheapest way to get to Lapland?
Be born there.

37

Mrs Tubby was dressing little Terry Tubby and told him he must wear lots of warm clothing to go out and play in the cold winter weather. 'Must I?' asked Terry. 'I hate wearing all these clothes.'

So Mrs Tubby told him a story about a little boy who went out to play with his sledge in the snow wearing just his shirt and jeans, and caught pneumonia and died. Terry sat listening open-mouthed. 'Oh, Mum,' he said when she'd finished, 'what happened to the sledge?'

HORACE: My grandad was a Pole.
DORIS: North or South?

GILL: How did you find the weather on your skiing holiday?
BILL: Oh, I just went outside and there it was.

DONNY: Can I have a go on your sledge?
RONNIE: Yes, we'll go halves.
DONNY: Thanks very much.
RONNIE: That's OK. I'll have it going downhill and you can have it going uphill.

Knock, knock.
Who's there?
Accordion.
Accordion who?
Accordion to the weather forecast it'll snow later.

Knock, knock.
Who's there?
Dawn.
Dawn who?
Dawn leave me standing out here in the snow.

What kind of fish is useful in icy weather?
A skate.

ROSY: You must have had good weather on your winter holiday – you've got a lovely tan.
POSY: No, it rained every day – that's rust!

What goes in pink and comes out blue?
A swimmer in winter.

Why don't spies like working on dark, cold winter days?
They can't see where their shadows are.

JOHNNY: There's one good thing about December fogs.
BONNIE: What's that?
JOHNNY: You can see what you're breathing.

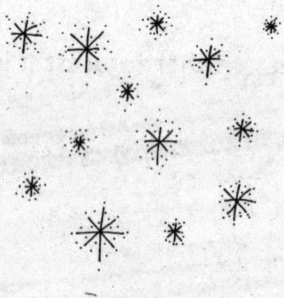

TALKING TURKEY

What happens if you cross a turkey with an octopus?
Every member of the family can have a leg.

What does a turkey become after it's nine months old?
Ten months old.

Where do you find wild turkeys?
That depends where you leave them.

Why is a turkey like an imp?
Because it's always a-gobblin'.

Why did the turkey cross the road?
To prove he wasn't chicken.

A mother turkey was scolding her naughty chicks. 'If your father were alive now he'd turn in his gravy,' she said.

BOBBY: Isn't it wonderful how little turkeys get out of their shells?
NOBBY: It's even more wonderful how they get into them!

Where do all good turkeys go when they die?
To oven.

JERRY: Should you eat turkey on an empty stomach?
KERRY: No, you should eat it on a plate.

On which side does a turkey have the most feathers?
The outside.

VICKY: We had roast boar for Christmas dinner.
MICKY: Was it wild?
VICKY: Well, it wasn't very pleased!

WAITER: And how did you find your turkey, sir?
DINER: Oh, I just moved a roast potato and there it was.

Did you hear the joke about the potatoes?
They didn't see eye to eye.

MOTHER: Eat your Brussels sprouts, they're good for growing children.
HASSAN: Who wants to grow children?

MOTHER: I've made the turkey soup.
HOLLY: Oh, good, I thought it was for us.

Why is Christmas pudding like the sea?
They're both full of currants.

What kind of wine do cannibals drink with Christmas dinner?
One with plenty of body.

What might you have on your Christmas
pudding that's yellow and dangerous?
Shark-infested custard.

How can you stop food going bad over
Christmas?
Eat it!

What are the best things to put in a Christmas
cake?
Your teeth!

MOTHER: Don't eat your mince pies so quickly!
MOLLY: But I might lose my appetite unless I do!

What do cats eat for Christmas breakfast?
Mice krispies.

What's round, green, smells fishy and is eaten
with Christmas dinner?
Brussels sprats.

Which is the left side of a Christmas pudding?
The piece that's left over.

What do hedgehogs eat for Christmas dinner?
Prickled onions.

The office Christmas lunch was held at a new
restaurant, and afterwards Arnie asked Barney
what he'd thought of it. 'Not much,' replied
Barney. 'It wasn't so much a restaurant as a
bureau of missing portions.'

On Christmas Day a mother said to her son,
'Now, Billy, we're having guests for dinner so I
want you to go upstairs and wash, change and
comb your hair and generally try to make
yourself look presentable.'

'Why?' asked Billy. 'Are you going to eat me for dinner?'

What does a lawyer put in his Christmas pudding?
Sue-t.

Why did the cook sit on the stove?
She felt at home on the range.

What did the cooker say to the saucepan?
'I can make things hot for you.'

FARMER: The hens have been drinking the Christmas whisky.
FARMER'S WIFE: How do you know?
FARMER: They're laying Scotch eggs.

MRS FEATHER: The turkey you sold me was very tough.
BUTCHER: Perhaps it hatched out of a hard-boiled egg.

Why couldn't one orange speak to the other orange on the phone?
The pips went.

What can a whole apple do that half an apple can't do?
Look round.

How do you make an apple turnover?
Push it off the table.

Why are grapes never lonely?
They hang around in bunches.

CUSTOMER AT FRUIT AND VEG STALL:
Who's in charge of the nuts?
STALLHOLDER: Hang on and I'll come and serve you in a moment.

48

Did you hear about the silly person who went to the fruit and veg stall?

He asked for 50g of mixed nuts, with not too many coconuts.

MRS TUBBY: I want to buy a nice Christmas cake, please.

CONFECTIONER: This is a nice one.

MRS TUBBY: It looks to me as if mice have nibbled it.

CONFECTIONER: Oh, no, that's impossible.

MRS TUBBY: How can you be so sure?

CONFECTIONER: Because the cat's been lying on it all day.

FRENCH CHEF: And how do our French dishes compare with your English ones?

ENGLISH CHEF: I'm afraid they break just as easily.

ANGRY MOTHER: This morning there were 12 mince pies in the larder and now there are only two. Why's that?
HER SON: I expect it's because it's so dark in there I didn't see the other two.

FIRST CANNIBAL: I just don't know what to make of my husband at this time of year.
SECOND CANNIBAL: How about a hotpot?

What did the cannibal do on his Christmas cruise?
Refused the menu and asked for the passenger list.

CHRIS, ON PHONE: Have you had your dinner yet?
HIS FRIEND: Yes, we were so hungry at 7.59 that we 8 o'clock.

GRANDAD: That turkey was very tough. I hope you're giving me something today that I can get my teeth into.
GRANDMA: Certainly, here's a glass of water.

CHRISTMAS DINER: May I finish with coffee without cream, please?
WAITER: Sorry, we're out of cream. Will you have it without milk?

DINER: This coffee tastes like mud!
WAITER: It was ground only a few minutes ago, sir.

WAITER: What will you have after your turkey, sir?
DINER: Indigestion, I expect, if it's anything like last year's.

What whirrs through the air and suffers from indigestion?
A bellycopter.

DINER: Waiter, you've got your thumb in my dinner.
WAITER: That's all right, sir, it isn't hot.

LADY IN RESTAURANT: May I join you?
SECOND LADY IN RESTAURANT: Why, am I coming apart?

LITTLE GIRL: Which hand should I use to stir my tea?
MOTHER: Neither, dear. Use a spoon.

What's the best way to cure acid indigestion?
Stop drinking acid.

Late on Christmas Eve a woman rushed into a butcher's to buy a turkey. The butcher only had one bird left, so he showed it to the customer. 'How much is it?' she asked.

'£10,' replied the butcher.

'Have you anything bigger?' she asked.

So the butcher took the turkey into the back room, plumped it up a bit and brought it back. 'This one is £12,' he said.

'That's fine,' said the customer. 'I'll take both of them.'

What did the fat man say as he sat down to Christmas dinner?
'I'm afraid all this food is going to waist.'

MRS TUBBY: I've eaten so much over Christmas I'm worried about losing my figure.
MRS SLIM: You'll have to diet.
MRS TUBBY: What colour?

MRS SMALL: Did you hear that Mrs Large has been on a crash diet?
MRS THYNNE: I thought she looked a complete wreck.

FREDDIE: Mum says she's going on a diet in the New Year.
TEDDY: Why?
FREDDIE: She says all this Christmas food has made her thick to her stomach.

What's a dieter's motto?
If at first you don't recede, diet again.

What do seven days of dieting do?
Make one weak.

JULIE: I'm going on a seafood diet.
JONIE: Seafood?
JULIE: Yes, the more I see food the more I eat it.

How can you make your Christmas cake light?
Pour paraffin over it.

JENNY: Try my Christmas cake.
JOHNNY: Yuck! It's horrible!
JENNY: You're quite wrong – the recipe says it's delicious.

LYNNE: Did you hear the joke about the heavyweight Christmas cake?
GWYN: No.
LYNNE: It takes some swallowing!

What jumps from cake to cake and tastes of almonds?
Tarzipan.

GILLY: I baked two Christmas cakes – take your pick.
BILLY: No thanks, I'll use my hammer.

MOTHER: What would you like for your tea?
BERTIE: Cake.
MOTHER: Cake what?
BERTIE: Cake first.

Which cake wanted to rule the world?
Attila the Bun.

What two things should you never eat before breakfast on Christmas Day?
Lunch and dinner.

Why did the idiot climb on to the restaurant roof when he went out for the office Christmas dinner?
He'd heard the meal was on the house.

FIRST DINER: This restaurant must have very clean kitchens.
SECOND DINER: Why do you say that?
FIRST DINER: All the food tastes of soap.

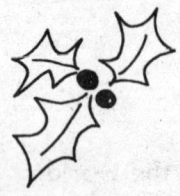

The family was getting ready for Christmas dinner. 'Have you put salt in the pot?' asked the mother.

'No,' replied her daughter. 'I couldn't get it through the little hole in the top of the pot.'

How do the Dumbos wash up after Christmas dinner?
Mrs Dumbo washes, Mr Dumbo dries and little Donald Dumbo picks up the pieces.

What did Hamlet say when he found he was putting on weight after Christmas?
'Tubby or not tubby, that is the question.'

What's the difference between a mince pie and a monster?
You can't eat a monster with your tea.

HARRY: Mum, are we going to Aunty Jane's on Boxing Day?
MOTHER: Yes, dear, we always do.
HARRY: Oh dear, I expect that means enthusiasm stew again.
MOTHER: What do you mean?
HARRY: She puts everything she's got into it.

Who has friends for Christmas dinner?
A cannibal.

PETER: Did you hear about the restaurant that had a special seasonal menu?
PAT: What was it?
PETER: Soup in a basket.

Mr Wide was late for Christmas dinner. He rushed into the house, and asked, 'Is my dinner still hot?'

'It should be,' replied his wife. 'It's been on the fire for the last half hour.'

Knock, knock.
Who's there?
Turkey Sam.
Turkey Sam who?
Turkey Sam Bridges for tea.

PARTY TIME

SANDRA: Will you come to our Christmas party?
EVANDER: Yes, please. Where do you live?
SANDRA: 26 Holly Avenue. It's the house on the corner. Just come up the steps and push the bell with your elbow.
EVANDER: Why with my elbow?
SANDRA: Well, you're not coming empty-handed, are you?

DOLLY: Do you like my dress? It's over 100 years old.
MOLLY: Did you make it yourself?

What game do monsters play at Christmas parties?
Swallow my leader.

What did the skeleton have at the Christmas party?
A rattling good time.

WALLY: I was going to wear a flower in my buttonhole at your party but I had to change my mind.
SALLY: Why's that?
WALLY: The flower pot kept hitting me in the stomach.

Alf and Ralph were going home after the Christmas party and they'd had rather too much to drink. 'Is that the sun or the moon?' asked Alf.

'I don't know,' replied Ralph. 'I don't live round here.'

ANGRY NEIGHBOUR: Didn't you hear me banging on your wall last night?
CALM NEIGHBOUR: Sorry, we were having a party and making quite a lot of noise ourselves.

KATIE: I was so embarrassed when they asked me to take off my mask at the New Year party.
KATHY: Why?
KATIE: I wasn't wearing one.

Did you hear about the girl who kissed a prince at a New Year party?
He turned into a toad.

Harold met Hamish at a New Year party. 'You're a Scotsman, aren't you,' he said.

'Aye,' answered Hamish.

'Well, what does "I dinna ken" mean?' asked Harold.

'I don't know,' replied Hamish.

'I thought you said you were a Scotsman!'

Knock, knock.
Who's there?
Juno.
Juno who?
Juno when the party starts?

MAN IN STREET: Can you tell me the time,
please? I've been invited to a Christmas party
and my watch isn't going.
PASSER-BY: Why, wasn't it invited too?

LITTLE JIMMY: Did you go to Terry's Christmas
party?
LITTLE TIMMY: No.
LITTLE JIMMY: Why not?
**LITTLE TIMMY: The invitation said from four to
seven and I'm eight.**

MOTHER: Did you thank Mrs Williams for the
lovely party?
**LITTLE SHARON: I was going to but when Karen
said, 'Thank you, Mrs Williams', Mrs Williams said,
'Don't mention it', so I didn't.**

A lady found a little boy crying in the street and asked him what was the matter. 'Oh,' he sobbed, 'I've just been to a lovely party. We had lots to eat, and presents, and a conjuror, and played games and it was wonderful.'

'Then why are you crying?' asked the lady.

'Because I'm lost,' wept the lad.

Where do ghosts go for a Christmas treat?
The phantomime.

Why was Cinderella thrown out of the football team?
She kept running away from the ball.

And why is she such a poor footballer?
Because her coach is a pumpkin.

Why did the horses visit the theatre?
They wanted to book a couple of stalls for the panto.

What pantomime is about a cat in a chemist's shop?
Puss in Boots.

What game do cows play at Christmas parties?
Moo sical chairs.

Where do cows go for a Christmas treat?
The moo-vies.

Why did the man crawl into the theatre?
Because he'd been told not to walk in late.

A theatre manager took his children to the
pantomime and was amazed to see an act with a
monkey playing the piano and a horse singing.
After the show he went round to the stage door
to speak to the producer. 'That act with the
monkey and the horse was fantastic!' he said. 'I'd
like to sign them up for a show at my theatre.
Come round to my office tomorrow and we'll
sign the contract.'

    The next morning the manager waited for the
producer, but he never turned up. So that
evening he went back to the theatre to find him.
'I'm sorry,' replied the producer, 'but I didn't
think I could go ahead with it. I wouldn't want to
cheat you. You see, it's all a bit of a fiddle. The
horse can't sing. The monkey is a ventriloquist.'

Knock, knock.
Who's there?
Fiona.
Fiona who?
Fiona had some money I could go to the
pantomime.

IVAN: I hear your brother has a leading position in the circus. What does he do?
RYAN: He leads in the elephants.

Why did the elephants leave the circus?
They were tired of working for peanuts.

Arnie and Barney had been to the circus. 'Did you have a good time?' asked Arnie's mum.

'Great!' said Arnie. 'But I didn't like the knife-thrower, did you, Barney?'

'No,' agreed Barney. 'He kept throwing knives at that stupid girl, but he didn't hit her once!'

OLLIE: What a terrifying film! It sent a shiver down my spine!
POLLY: So that's where my ice cream went.

Bryn took Lyn to the cinema for a treat. 'Can you see all right?' he asked.

'Yes, fine,' she replied.

'Your seat's comfortable?'

'Yes, very,' said Lyn.

'And there's no one blocking your view?'

'No, everything's fine.'

'Mind changing places then?'

MR DIM: Did you go to Spain for Christmas?
MR DUMB: I don't know, my wife bought the tickets.

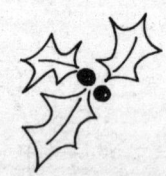

MRS KELLY: So you're not going to Scotland for New Year this year?
MRS NELLY: No, it's Wales we're not going to this year. It was Scotland we didn't go to last year.

MR HIRD: Did you enjoy the scenery when you went skiing in Switzerland?
MR NERD: We didn't see much of it, there were too many mountains in the way.

What happened when Mr and Mrs Careful went skiing?
They wouldn't go out until the slopes had been gritted.

BELLE: Have you ever been water-skiing?
DEL: No, I've never managed to find a sloping lake.

CAROL: Hugh's family are sending him to his penfriend's for Christmas.
DARRYL: Does he need a holiday?
CAROL: No, but his parents do.

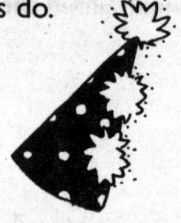

The Dumble family were thinking of spending Christmas on a farm as they'd had such a good time there in the summer. But then Mrs Dumble remembered how the pigs had smelt, so she rang up the farmer to ask if the pigs were still there.

'No,' he replied, 'we haven't had any pigs on the farm since you were here last summer.'

DENNIS: I learnt one thing over the Christmas holidays – that TV really does cause violence.
DORIS: How did you learn that?
DENNIS: Because every time I switched it over my brother hit me.

Why did Jemima stand on a ladder when she was singing in the school carol concert?
So she could reach the high notes.

The youngest class at school were drawing the nativity scene, and little Susie had put in the manger, the ox, the ass and the shepherds. 'And what's that thing in the corner?' asked her teacher.

'That?' said Susie. 'That's their television.'

MOTHER: Why don't you like your teacher?
MILLY: She told me to sit in the front row for the present, but she didn't give me a present.

Just after Christmas the school doctor was giving vaccinations. He was about to put a plaster on one boy's arm when the lad said, 'Can you put it on the other arm, please?'

'But I'm covering up your vaccination so the other boys at school won't bump into it,' explained the doctor.

'You don't know the boys at my school,' explained the lad ruefully.

MOTHER: And were you well behaved at the carol service?
DEREK: Oh, yes. And when that nice lady offered me a plateful of money I said no thank you.

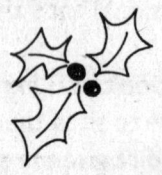

MERRY CHRISTMAS, AND A HAPPY NEW YEAR!

Which is the hardest train to catch on
Christmas Eve?
The 12.50, because it's ten to one if you catch it.

What happens if you eat the Christmas
decorations?
You get tinselitis.

Who wrote *Christmas Decorations*?
Holly Wreath and Miss L. Toe.

What do ghosts hang on their doors at
Christmas?
Holly wraiths.

How does Jack Frost get to work?
By icicle.

What did the woodman's wife say?
'Not many chopping days to Christmas.'

POST OFFICE CLERK: You've put too many stamps on this Christmas card.
CUSTOMER: Oh dear, it won't go too far, will it?

What illness do spies get in midwinter?
A code in the nose.

What's a robin?
A bird that burgles.

'Why are you wearing your socks to paddle?'
'The water's cold in December.'

What did the Christmas cracker say to its friend?
'My pop's bigger than your pop.'

What lives in winter, grows with its roots upwards and dies in summer?
An icicle.

What makes a Christmas
tree noisy?
Its bark.

What will happen to
you at Christmas?
Yule be happy.

How many famous
people were born on
Christmas Day?
None, only babies.

MR WIMP: I've felt half dead since Christmas.
**DR WUMP: I'll arrange for you to be buried up to
your waist.**

What's the difference between influenza and
photography?
One makes sick families; the other facsimiles.

FIRST MUSICIAN: I swallowed my flute at
Christmas.
**SECOND MUSICIAN: Be glad you don't play the
piano.**

GARY: I had a narrow squeak on Christmas Day.
BARRY: What happened?
GARY: I trod on a mouse.

Mrs Long knocked on Mrs Short's door on Boxing Day and said, 'I hope you don't mind me mentioning it but I've noticed that every morning you hit your son with a slice of toast.'

'That's right,' said Mrs Short.

'But yesterday you hit him with a piece of cake,' said Mrs Long. 'Why?'

'Well, yesterday was Christmas Day,' replied Mrs Short.

CLARK: When we got up on Christmas morning we found a helicopter on the roof.
MARK: Why?
CLARK: When Dad was filling our stockings he left the landing light on.

What do you call someone who breaks into the pantry and steals the Christmas gammon?
A hamburglar.

Why can't you hide a
Christmas tree?
Its bark gives it away.

WILLIAM: Will you kiss
me under the mistletoe?
**WENDY: I'd rather kiss
you under the nose.**

What do sad Christmas trees do?
They pine a lot.

How do you tell the time by
the Christmas
candles?
By the candles' tick.

How do you tell a pair
of golf socks from a pair
of Christmas stockings?
**The golf socks usually have
a hole in one.**

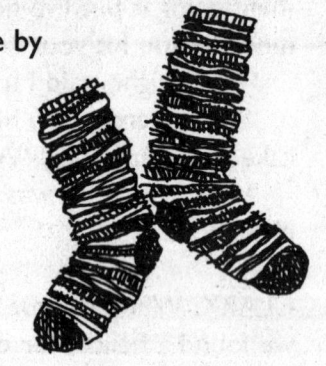

Chris went to Australia for Christmas and when
he returned he showed his friends his holiday
pictures. One showed Chris having a ride on a
donkey on the beach. 'I like your photos but
who's that on your back?' asked one of his
friends.

Jeff was late on his first morning back at work
after the Christmas break. 'Why are you late?'
asked his boss.

'I'm sorry,' said Jeff, 'but the bus was late.'

'Well, if it's late again tomorrow you'll have to
catch an earlier one.'

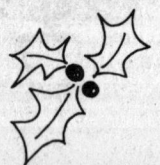

On Christmas Eve the police station received a call from a stately home to say that a thief had stolen six paintings, some silver candlesticks, some antique china and a pair of trousers.

'Did you chase the thief?' asked the constable.

'No,' replied the caller. 'They were my trousers.'

Did you hear about the silly person who decided to have his sundial floodlit for Christmas? He wanted to be able to tell the time by it at night.

What do you call a tug of war on 24 December?
Christmas 'eave.

MRS COUCH-POTATO: What's on the TV this Christmas?
MR COUCH-POTATO: Same as usual, a bowl of fruit and a vase of flowers.

Why is Christmas Day never complete?
Because it begins by breaking.

TEACHER: Ronnie, are you late again? I thought you said you were having an alarm clock for Christmas?
RONNIE: I did, but it keeps going off when I'm asleep.

What's green, spiky and goes slam, slam, slam, slam?
A four-door Christmas tree.

What do you call ten ducks in a crate on 24 December?
A box of Christmas quackers.

Why are Christmas trees always warm?
Because they're fir trees.

What do gorillas sing at Christmas?
'Jungle bells, jungle bells . . .'

What's Christmas called in Great Britain?
Yule Britannia.

Why is a cat on a beach like Christmas?
Because of its sandy claws.

Did you hear about the couple who met in a revolving door at the January sales?
They're still going around together.

A passenger who wanted to travel to Rome by train at Christmas rang a travel agent to ask how long the journey would be. 'Just a minute,' replied the travel agent.

'Thanks very much,' said the caller, and hung up.

PASSENGER: How long will the next train be?
TICKET COLLECTOR: Two carriages if it's the local, 12 if it's the Inter-City.

What do you get if you
cross a snowman with a
man-eating shark?
Frostbite.

What goes, 'Now you see me, now you don't, now you see me, now you don't'?
A snowman walking over a zebra crossing.

BOSS, INTERVIEWING JOB APPLICANT: We need people to cut down Christmas trees – they must be able to cut down at least 100 trees a day.
JOB APPLICANT: You need me, I'm a good feller.

VAL: One Christmas when I was young my mother almost lost me.
CAL: She probably didn't take you far enough into the woods.

What's the difference between an iced lolly and the stamp you stick on a Christmas card?
One you lick with a stick, the other you stick with a lick.

What do spacemen do when they spend Christmas in space?
Play astronauts and crosses.

Why is this Christmas card damp?
Maybe there's postage dew.

MOTHER: Who was that on the phone?
DAUGHTER: Oh, just someone who said it was a
long distance from Australia, but I said I already
knew that.

Where do snowmen
dance?
At snowballs.

CHAS: What are you doing?
BAZ: Writing a Christmas card to myself.
CHAS: What does it say?
BAZ: I won't know until I get it tomorrow.

Who wrote *Christmas Worship*?
Neil Downe.

Who wrote *Happy Christmas*?
Trudi Light.

Where can you post your Christmas cards when you're asleep?
In a pillow box.

What did the crocodile say to the giraffe?
'Hippo Christmas!'

HIL: We went to Paris for Christmas and climbed the Eiffel Tower.
PHIL: What did you see?
HIL: Quite an eyeful.

On Christmas Day silly Billy climbed a tree and couldn't get down again. 'Can't you get down the same way you went up?' called his brother.
    'Oh, no,' said Billy. 'I came up head first.'

JOHNNY: At Christmas my sister threw pepper in my face.
DONNY: What did you do?
JOHNNY: I sneezed.

Knock, knock.
Who's there?
Snow.
Snow who?
Snow use, I've forgotten my key.

Knock, knock.
Who's there?
Waiter.
Waiter who?
Waiter minute while I put my scarf on, it's cold out there.

Knock, knock.
Who's there?
Jimmy.
Jimmy who?
Jimmy a kiss under the mistletoe.

What do you get if you cross a polar bear with a kangaroo?
A fur coat with pockets.

What do you get if you cross a sheep with a rainstorm?
A wet blanket.

Why does Father sit with his mouth open after Chrismas dinner?
He's so lazy it saves him having to open it to yawn.

What begins with P, ends with E, has lots of letters in between and is very useful at Christmas?
Post office.

DARREN: Have you many church bells in your town?
SHARON: About 100, all tolled.

JAYNE: The choir master said I had a heavenly voice.
WAYNE: No he didn't, he said it was like nothing on earth.

ADAM: Did you notice how my voice filled the church?
ALAN: Yes, and did you notice how many people left to make room for it?

Little Tessa was sitting by the fire on Christmas Eve playing with her kitten when the kitten started to purr. 'Mum,' she shouted, 'come quickly! I think the kitten's boiling!'

DAVE: I was given a canary for Christmas and I lost it. What should I do?
MAEVE: Contact the Flying Squad.

FATHER: All the bills go up at Christmas – the gas, the phone, the food bills – why doesn't anything come down?
SON: Er, Dad, here are my exam results.

What cakes would children *not* like for Christmas?
Cakes of soap.

SURESH: What a nice hat. Was it a Christmas present?
SIMON: Yes. It's a hunting hat.
SURESH: Why do you call it a hunting hat?
SIMON: Because my brother got it for Christmas and he'll be hunting for it!

HUSBAND: Would you like
a pair of crocodile shoes
for Christmas?
**WIFE: No, thanks, I never
wear secondhand clothes.**

HUSBAND: Were the shops crowded at the
sales?
**WIFE: Yes, so crowded I saw two women trying on
the same dress.**

JULIET: Why did you buy me
such a small diamond?
**ROMEO: I didn't want the glare
to hurt your eyes.**

Two days after Christmas an angry mother went
into a toyshop and demanded her money back.
'This unbreakable toy is useless,' she said.

'But your child can't have broken it already,'
replied the assistant.

'No,' agreed the mother. 'But he's broken all
his other toys with it.'

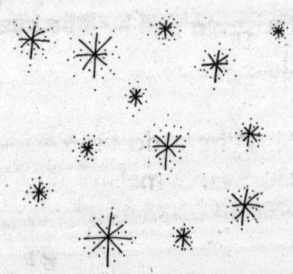

Knock, knock.
Who's there?
Java.
Java who?
Java good Christmas?

Knock, knock.
Who's there?
Wendy.
Wendy who?
Wendy red, red robin comes bob, bob,
bobbin' along.

Knock, knock.
Who's there?
Gin.
Gin who?
Gingle bells, gingle bells . . .

What has the shortest lifespan?
A New Year resolution. It is born before
midnight and dead and forgotten the following
day.

Why is 2004 a good year for kangaroos?
It's a leap year.

RYAN: Where do fleas go in winter?
BRYAN: Search me!

Two dragons were discussing their New Year resolutions. 'I think,' said the first, 'that this year I really will try to give up smoking.'

What do cats strive for in their New Year resolutions?
Purr-fection.

KELLY: Do you think this is a good photo of me?
NELLY: Well, it makes you look older.
KELLY: It'll save me having another one done next year.

SIGN IN A STATIONERY SHOP WINDOW: Calendars and diaries – all with one year's guarantee.

SIGN OUTSIDE A NEW SHOP: Don't go anywhere else to be robbed – try us first.

Bryan had New Year flu. He asked his doctor, 'How can I avoid this run-down feeling?'
   'Look both ways before crossing the street,' suggested his doctor.

GILES: What have you done for your cold?
MILES: Nothing.
GILES: Why not?
MILES: It hasn't done anything for me!

SCOTT: What did your doctor suggest when you asked him how to get fit?
WAT: He suggested I should exercise with a dumb-bell. Will you come to the gym with me?

Knock, knock.
Who's there?
Godfrey.
Godfrey who?
Godfrey tickets for the panto!

Knock, knock.
Who's there?
Noah.
Noah who?
Noah good place to spend Christmas?

Knock, knock.
Who's there?
Europe.
Europe who?
Europe early this Christmas morning.

Knock, knock.
Who's there?
Police.
Police who?
Police let me in, it's snowing.

Knock, knock.
Who's there?
Luke.
Luke who?
Luke out for Santa on Christmas Eve.

Knock, knock.
Who's there?
Mary.
Mary who?
Mary Christmas!

MERRY CHRISTMAS!